TREMULOUS HINGE

Winner of the Iowa Poetry Prize

TREMULOUS HINGE

Poems by ADAM GIANNELLI

University of Iowa Press, Iowa City

University of Iowa Press, Iowa City 52242
Copyright © 2017 by Adam Giannelli
All rights reserved
www.uipress.uiowa.edu
Printed in the United States of America

Design by Barbara Haines

The University of Iowa Press is a member of Green Press Initiative and is committed to preserving natural resources.

Printed on acid-free paper

Library of Congress Cataloging-in-Publication Data
Names: Giannelli, Adam, author.
Title: Tremulous hinge : poems / by Adam Giannelli.
Description: Iowa City : University of Iowa Press, [2017] | Series: Iowa poetry prize |
Includes bibliographical references.
Identifiers: LCCN 2016040302 | ISBN 978-1-60938-486-9 (pbk) |
ISBN 978-1-60938-487-6 (ebk)
Classification: LCC PS3607.I2236 A6 2017 | DDC 811/.6—dc23
LC record available at https://lccn.loc.gov/2016040302

*Though it is true
that fire is the enemy of water,
moist heat is the creator of all things*

—Ovid

CONTENTS

ACKNOWLEDGMENTS

Grateful acknowledgment is made to the editors of the following publications where versions of these poems first appeared: *American Literary Review*, "Plea for Interlude"; *Antioch Review*, "On a Line by Proust," "Hush"; *Cincinnati Review,* "Rain"; *Colorado Review*, "Orchids, Avenues"; *Confrontation*, "Perch" (formerly "Epilogue"); *Ecotone*, "The Shards Still Trembling"; *FIELD*, "Incurable Cloud"; *Kenyon Review,* "Fern and Shadow," "Garland," "The Opposite of Sugar"; *Kenyon Review Online*, "Porcupine"; *Missouri Review Online*, "The String"; *New England Review*, "Sealevel," "Clearing, Clear"; *Ploughshares*, "Stutter"; *Smartish Pace*, "The Phone Call," "What We Know"; *Southwest Review*, "A Thousand Small Nights"; *32 Poems*, "How the Light Is Spent," "Curl"; *Virginia Quarterly Review Online*, "Late Audience"; *Water-Stone*, "The Brunt of Love," "Passage"; *West Branch*, "My Insomnia," "Gravity"; *Yale Review*, "Little Winds," "Half the Leaves."

"What We Know" is anthologized in *Best New Poets 2009* (Samovar/Meridian, 2009).

I would like to thank my teachers, friends, and colleagues for their counsel, attention, and encouragement, especially Adam Atkinson, Malachi Black, Tommye Blount, Marianne Boruch, Dan Chaon, Maria Chelko, Katharine Coles, Martha Collins, Rita Dove, Katherine Larson, Gregory Orr, Jacqueline Osherow, Paisley Rekdal, Jerry Rosco, Lisa Russ Spaar, Charles Wright, and David Young.

I am indebted to the following organizations, without whose help this book would not have been possible: University of Utah, University of Virginia, Oberlin College, James Merrill House, Bread Loaf Writers' Conference for a Carol Houck Smith Scholarship, Sewanee Writers'

Conference for a Tennessee Williams Scholarship, Tyrone Guthrie Centre, Vermont Studio Center for a James Merrill Fellowship, Ragdale Foundation, Djerassi Artist Program, Ucross Foundation, and Virginia Center for the Creative Arts.

Thanks to Craig Morgan Teicher for believing in this manuscript, and thanks to James McCoy and everyone at the University of Iowa Press for helping to make this book possible.

Finally, I am grateful to my family, especially Paul, Susan, and Michael Giannelli, Neil Giannelli, and Sonia Lugo, for their love and devotion.

Stutter

since I couldn't say *tomorrow*
I said *Wednesday*

since I couldn't say *Cleveland* I said
Ohio
       since I couldn't say *hello*

I hung up
since I couldn't say *burger*

a waitress finished
my sentence

       a green-striped mint
          dissolved

       on my tongue
       from peacock to dove

since I couldn't say my name
         I opened

       as if preparing for a throat
       culture

since I couldn't say my name
       I sat there

since I couldn't say *water*
I drank

        I could speak as camouflage
        as in a Greek play or firing squad

        so I stood in a row and pledged
            allegiance in chorus

since I couldn't say *dynamite*
my mother
drove me to hearing and speech

each Tuesday
            since she knew
I couldn't say *butter the bread*

        she stopped on the way
        home for Italian ice at Corbo's

        since I couldn't say *pistachio*
        I ordered *hazelnut*

I could say vowels so
I said *easy does it*

        I always said *easy does it*
        I said
            all aboard

since I can't say *everlasting*
I say *every*
            lost thing

alone in my room I can
speak any word

since I can't say *memory* I say
underbloom

and under me
a mulberry tree

a puddle shorn from the storm

Fern and Shadow

This severed earth, a veined vapor.
Its name is *prunes easily in water*. Its name—
fern and shadow. An understudy,

                porous.

On the subway, I hear the others lap
against their collars. Eyes
closed, elbows to knees, a woman
holds her head

           aloft in her hand.

Lifting up his shirt, a man removes
a bandage from a rash.

               Faithfully, it bleeds.

These arms that coil at night, a nest,
unravel in the morning,

             a narrative.

This apology. Asked to clench or coax,
read or ruffle,

         to burrow or bury.

This freight. Call it a *body*,

           if that helps you.

Sealevel

Last night I went back and removed all the angels
from my poems.
I singed their wings
               and gave them names.
Now they wander the beach at Rockaway,
sunburned, far from home.
They fan out a towel in the breeze
or lie until sweat
               alights on their foreheads.

This close to Kennedy, the planes fly
low enough for us to see the colors of the rudders.
One crosses overhead,
               leaving a white girder in the sky.
You say, *But I thought TWA went out of business.*

Scintillate with white grit, the waves
fall one after another—
               a perpetual curtain call.
It's easy to say one word, *field* or *flower*, even *geranium*,
but *upright* is two words yoked together.
Say it in one breath; *home*
               still falls before *sick,*
sun before *down.*
On the horizon, sails, white bevels, glide.

On our way to the bus, we squeeze paper cups
so that lemon ice
                    slopes over the rim.
A group of men corral dominoes on a table.
On the citronella candle, a flame glistens
like the tip of a paintbrush
                            dipped in amber.
It fans out, flattened in the wind,
                                    brush on canvas—

Star Gazers

The way we look at the stars,
    the stars look at us, and make
constellations—not of our lives, skittish, but our deaths, dark
   and steadfast. In the morning,
     beneath a bedspread or under
a bridge, each exit intrudes, an island in

   an archipelago of shadow,
     and the stars have a game of it,
divining a pitchfork, a painter's easel, a wagon, a conglomeration
   called Madeline's hair.
     But sometimes the stars are hasty—
for months a man lies in St. Vincent's after

   an intracerebral hemorrhage,
     hardly moving, except to change
the channel of a television in the corner or ask the priest
   to leave. Although faint,
     he's lined up in a row with three others
in his wing to form the lip of a cup.

   The stars look and draw
     the constellation, its points,
in their almanacs, and then embellish it with emanating beams.
   They tell stories of how the cup
     was lost, and sought by knights. The man
rises, once a day, from bed and, clutching

parallel bars, tries to walk
in a room of mirrors. His point
of the constellation wavers, and some insist he's a planet.
Eventually, he lets go for three
steps, then for five. Before the mirror,
he rehearses greeting loved ones and strangers,

and soon he's walking down
Christopher Street towards the Hudson—
the diameter of the cup widening, farther and farther, beyond all
proportion. *That's just a satellite,*
says one star. *No, no,* says another.
It's too fast. Look at it falling across the earth.

Hydrangea

Water vessel—patina of summer—
its zeppelins soar all the way
into September, the heads colored
like the flavored ice atop snow cones. Beside a driveway and a house,
a few orbs, flamingo-like, float
on thin stalks. Others, laden
with bloom, rest, like tails of tired poodles, on the ground.

Each mophead is a bevy, a beveled
blue, a standing ovation,
that fumes with lattices of spume, solid but fretful, like sleep.
I never knew that ecstasy
could arrive at
so many angles. These breakers
compass an entire globe. Coming to fisticuffs, each scrub

clenches nebula and knuckle—its bicep
bulges, its big kahunas, composed
of a chorus of florets, cups of three or four petals, flaring sepals
that abut like umbrellas,
or moths all swarming the
same light bulb. Like a cloud formation
touching ground, the hydrangea offers no conclusion,

only a deckled edge—and flocks toward
the edges, coveting coastal climes, shade-wrangled soil, dappled light.
Rilke wrote two poems,
but you hold blue and pink
in the same body. Your blooms, pigment-
pliant, can change, from one year to the next, from salmon to mauve
to blue. Bearded lady,

balloon man, chameleon. You make of yourself
shoreline, ebbing and eddying with creams, cobalts—or mosaic,
piecing together lavender and lilac—and so insist that
where there is gradation,
there is bounty. I learned
from you to place the most generous part first, to complicate always
with yet another

fold, to contain more than one name.
The distinctions between one cultivar and another are so faint
that confronted with a single plant's corrugations,
its swath of lily pads,
it can be near impossible to surmise its name—Blue Bonnet,
Hamburg, Seascape—Ave Maria.
You can be willed

more blue, or coaxed toward
pink, so that your florals become not predestined but a destination.
With aluminum sulfate in your soil, you blue,
and, with lime, blush.
Rabid for reds, I station a plant, because of the lime in cement,
beside a concrete path and watch as it
bursts into flames.

A tulip is singular,
solar, on its stem, but you honeycomb
and bouquet. Powder blue and pink spheres can appear on the same
shrub, so that, a solar system, it holds within
its sway a Mars and Venus. And there floats
a single orb, amidst
revision, half blue,

half pink, marbled, nursing the shades
from dawn to high noon, proliferating with roiling waters, airy inlets,
continents, craters, peninsulas of cloud,
converting, like a bivalve shell, difference, beyond
mere border, into the cradle of a vast
and viscous muscle—
all to make more dutifully a world.

How the Light Is Spent

Even the light accepts the trespasses
against it, so that a bit of shade

chars the grass. Across the gravel
at the underpass
                        it makes a clean break,

but more often it ends in a mottle
of amber and umber.
                        The bevels of

leaves become the light's ambivalences—
and below, the veil.

In the spokes of a bicycle, it
pulsates, and between the loiterers

by the taco stand,
                        erects pillars.
Beneath the maples it concedes whole

realms that house any leaves that
may fall.
                There are places it won't go—

the sea floor, the ingot of shadow
in a drawer. Like a visitor in a hospital

it waits, warming the spot off
to one side—and it takes such lengths

to leave the room, lingering at
the bedside,
                    the far wall, the doorjamb.

Porcupine

Into pelt and sheen, rattans bond, tight-
slatted. At rest, sheaved
    from the front, it is wickerwork, canebrake,
        quiver of arrows, but when
provoked it erupts as bayonets, asterisk, threshing floor,
        Cupid in a fury.

    Its strategy is not precision, but exuberance—
        a briery boast. Let the arrows fly—
gold with lead. Florescent-
    quilled, in dark makeup, like the bass player
        in an 80s band, it announces its eccentricity—
then fades, making meager

    its own spotlight. But no porcupine can shoot
its quills, so as in any romance, its
        pierce depends on flair and
proximity. Maligned by lumberjacks and commuters alike,
        it has been maimed, poisoned,
    and shotgun-blared. They do not

accommodate you—your salt drive,
        your night-sleuthing, your implacable whiskers.
    But we all have unlidded nights; we all have
thorns. The same gaze that forgets
        the rose's quills makes a bonfire
    out of yours. But thorniness

is no more than an erratic
smooth. Your paws are polished
                and pebbled. The underside
of your tail, mildly bristled to gain
                purchase as it barnacles in the branches. Above the tail
                appears a bald spot with shorter barbs—

a meadow, a rosette that, like an open
flower, broadcasts a pungent aroma—a warning that
                accompanies the splayed quills.
I choose you, my escaped
convict—you run with your stripes still on you.
                Although you're slow and nearsighted,

when you unveil your ribbons, fantailed, I feel
                as though I am entering
lightspeed. From out of the bare serene, the stars
                all striate—and you arch in monochrome,
like a rainbow above
                a distant hill in a silent film.

My Insomnia

My insomnia enfolds
itself like an ear and lies
  for a long time, listening in the dark. Or falls to its back—
    rigid as a shelf of coral. The only
difference, my insomnia reasons, between its own predicament
    and fasting is resolve.
      Slipping a hand beneath

  the pillow, my insomnia
abuts the cold. Some nights
  my insomnia holds a flashlight under the covers—
    not to conceal the light,
but to reduce the visible world to an amenable gleam. My insomnia
    is an avid reader, and calls
      the bed *Robinson's Island*, and

  the pillow, *Friday*. My insomnia
writes poetry, but confined
  to a world of light and dark is prone to melodrama.
    My insomnia has its pride,
and never stoops to espresso or methamphetamine. It rolls out of bed,
    forward and unrepentant,
      into dusky latencies.

My insomnia suspects
that sleep is a form
of genuflection. It drags a chair through the lawn and basks
in the moonlight, convinced that
the constellations are slowly sliding past each other like tectonic plates.
It delights in crosswalks,
pinball machines, snowplows,

and anything else with
a checkered glow. It likes
to drive, although it has never heard the sound of traffic.
My insomnia takes the car
out on the highway past the city's nimbus, where the landscape would
be unintelligible if not
for place names.

Once it wanted to visit
an aquarium, but had to settle
for a casino with live dolphins. Defined by a lack,
my insomnia shies away from
its own name, but is yet to arrive at another. At the mention of sleep,
my insomnia pretends
to understand. Confronted

with the slow quake of
others slumbering nearby,
my insomnia lets them drowse, sad to discover that sleep
contains its own fits and
vociferous cries. Despite such intimacies, my insomnia remains a virgin.
As it brushes its teeth,
it wonders if it is ticklish.

My insomnia looks into
the windows of restaurants
          after they've closed, when the chairs, like a herd of elk,
                    are stacked atop the tables—
each distinguished by its antlers. It peers into an antique store, inside
          of which a solitary light
                    abides, suffusing the sherbet glasses

          and amber bowls. My insomnia
has returned several times
          to see the same porcelain vase. It regards warm baths,
                    chamomile, and Ambien as bribes,
but receives them out of politeness. Sometimes my insomnia lies
          with its feet on the pillow—
                    not out of irreverence but

          desperation. My insomnia
asks me what falling
          asleep is like. I say, *like your shoelaces loosening.*
                    Once my insomnia started to
drift away, but could not bring itself to part with a spider in the corner
                    adding more white lilacs
                              to a flimsy bouquet.

Late Audience

in a lavish sweat
across a bed with
one sheet while

the wind carries
its empty package
through the streets

on one of those
nights when you've
come home and

still dressed lie
down beneath
the ceiling fan's

quiet knell
for who knows
how long

a lamp in the corner
left spewing its
stubborn bright

the first blackbirds
rummaging
in the wet grass

trying to skirt
the darkness with
their calls

when listening
to them
is enough

Garland

The glass on the bureau can anything be seen
on the bottom? Is it filled

                        with water or milk
or nothing? The dog who lost his hair
has he grown it back

                 or gone bald?
He lies in the corner.

                 Is he cold or just quiet?
The woman by the window are her lips pursed
or parted? Is she drinking

                 or humming?
Is the necklace fastened around her neck
or folded in her hand?

                 Is it a circle or a strand?
The two young men strolling past the marquee
are their hands fused

                 or flitting by their sides?
Do they resemble dew

                 or drift? The sky pink
and waning. Am I lost

                 or have I been lifted?

The String

If a circle is what you're after, you must
make a knot. If tautness,

                pull.

It begins—

        a band of cream, the sash
of steaming windows on the fifty-seven bus

in the rain, the edge of spume that fizzles
over the sand at Rockaway after each wave

rumbles then retreats—

                cumulus then stratus.

In the morning you step out the front door
and squint—the ocean inside

breaking—a single plume,

                aria, tendril.

You decide whether to pull the line—
drawing back a curtain or wafting a kite

in the half-breeze—, to thread it through
ice skates at Flushing Meadows,

or wind it into a coil around itself
—nautilus, ribbon—, or fold it over

the edge of a knife

              and cut it in half.

The Brunt of Love

I've seen the word garnish the bottom
of my letters. I've heard it
spoken early, before the pawnshops
roll up their iron gates and the sun rises
bald and blood-colored, before
the mouth is bitten, washed with salt water, and left
a listless harbor. But moments come

when circumstance sets our affections, flushed
and swollen, in absurd relief, against
blankets, bars of soap, or the incandescence
of Mercy Hospital: a wilderness
in the blood. First, she suffered a stroke—
then grandfather dislocated his back
lifting her wheelchair into the trunk of a Cadillac.

Along Woodhaven, the maples emit
shades of yellow and green,
like unripe limes. A siren bores through cold air.
My eyes are bloodshot, as if set
in small cages. I sent bouquets of tulips, daisy mums,
then tea and dried apricots
when he could no longer lift the vase.

Orchids, Avenues

At the skate park, the ramps reiterate
the chafe of polyurethane. Trash cans

teem with wet paper, candy wrappers.
A basketball net hangs—
                              a punctured sieve.

Early in the morning when the buses run
by the hour, a dampness

covers the grass and pavement. I walk
and walk. It cannot
                              be stamped out.

I never found that one place that waited,
like a bell untolling. That person whose ardor

had no eyelids. At the bridge over the railing
I reach out my arm.
                              It slopes.

When someone enters the dry cleaners,
the bell above the door chimes,

and an old man emerges from the linens.
Brutal how time
                      is as our only trellis.

A woman walks to work in a navy skirt
and heels. Her footsteps

                chatter like teeth.

In the empty band shell, paint curls
from the edges

              of the benches. A motor idles.

Little Winds

for Benedict Egan, 1918–2013

The cars on Sunrise
reduce to headlights.

Above the King Kullen
the stars resume

their old staring contest.

     * * * * *

Residence turned
to reticence.

     * * * * *

In 1974 you published
The Four C's of …

Outdoor Advertising.

I wonder about
your ellipsis.

     * * * * *

Copy—

In your old age
the mailbox became

for you an event.

＊＊＊＊＊

I shall conclude, you wrote
at the end of a letter.

The archaism was not

meant to be prophetic
but ambitious.

You never went to college.

＊＊＊＊＊

In your letters too,
ellipses

rise like midges.

＊＊＊＊＊

Coverage—

Shore Road in Bay Ridge,
Lüchow's at Christmas,

the Rockville Links (you

were their first Catholic),
Montauk lighthouse,

the house on Roxen Road

where the third step from
the bottom of the staircase

would sound the alarm.

. . . . .

All these years
I was hesitant to break

away from the coals,

and now the coals
have broken
                from me.

. . . . .

At the liquor store
we get boxes to

disembowel the rooms.

. . . . .

Circulation—

Because of heavy snow,
my mother's flight

landed in Allentown.

As she traveled by taxi
to the hospital,

you kept coursing.

        * * * * *

The candles on a cake
reflect in your glasses.

In each photo a flame

of one sort or another lilts—
and your image is

the irreparable ash.

        * * * * *

The leaves in the grass
bend into
        little boats—

The elms are black
easels.

        * * * * *

Continuity—

I think your punctuation,

a star field of dots, dashes,
is because of the billboards—

anything to stand out

against a white facade
to speeding passersby.

—This rage I know.

＊ ＊ ＊ ＊ ＊

Even your pamphlet,

with those dashes,
ends in a wreath—

to i-m-p-e-l and s-e-l-l.

＊ ＊ ＊ ＊ ＊

We wait on the sod for
the bagpipes,

since you had ordered them

for your eldest son,
and

for your wife.

Aspens in Wind

each leaf   pried from shadow   glittering

like aspirins   dissolving in water

obliged to a branch and shot   of arrow   saint sebastians

turning and tethered   quivering   then quiet

to be leaf   rise into   toil over

to believe   to flit from sparrow   to sparrow

to herald from   within   and then

hang   less than green   withholding

brown   trembling   and giving tremble

like bathers   at shirley lake treading   water

the difference between *fall*   and *falter*

father and *falter*   so I skipped stones across

the surface   and counted   the splashes

these eyes like seeds this gaze   foliage

and foiled by age   heckled from one shore

to another   or sinking   falling to shadow

shadow falling   to leaf   like two hands clasping

to unleaf   unleaven   leave

Passage

for Marjorie C. Giannelli, 1916–2000

Clouds thin to their bones.
They sit but don't eat. Napkins
tumble to the floor.

The elms are stitched
with white and unravel
again. On the street

snow, just fallen,
is latticed by tire tracks.
Nurses fold sheets, but

there's nothing to harness.
Absence isn't clear—
it's a fine powder.

It falls and lingers for days—
a teacup, striations of letters,
an unplugged television.

On the grass, clumps of snow,
like crumbs on a blouse,
refuse to scatter.

I throw salt on the pavement—
my breath conspicuous
in the cold, and watch

neighbors bring in groceries
as the sky darkens.
—Not lost without a way

but a way is lost. The old oak
barnacled with ice.
O moon, you've made

a hole out of white.

Sweet Imposition

Like sea foam, it gathers atop the fences
and rests there, silent and lofty. The inverse
of shadow, it's not a figment
below, but a froth up above—a heavenly jetsam.

It lends, like ointment, a polish to the fire hydrants
and trash bins, the bicycle inclined against
an elm. Along the street, the cars
have carapaces, and the window ledges,

like book easels, display white pages. A spruce,
bulbous, is a coral reef. Across the earth lies
a ghostly overlay that won't
be revived, only wished upon, or brushed away.

—The body of water by the house where
you lived was called the Sound, meaning channel,
but to me it always referred
to the water's din, a slow lapping that unlike

the ocean's rupture and recuperation,
formed a constant reverberation, a sound. The rocks
along the beach, less battered,
were coarser than the sand's distillation—

and you were coarser, who mailed me brownies
inside of a shoebox, and laughed when I was afraid
of the German shepherd,
your lone companion, who reached my nose.

One day you confessed that you had lost the dog—
a prelude to other losses: Thanksgiving, the way
into town, how to comb
hair, my name, and eventually your coarseness

itself. Instead of *janitor*, you look up
from a plastic tray and say, *the man who cleans*. I think
of that house in Riverhead,
the fireman's helmet on the wall. The flakes fall.

Curl

Each leaf is a width of water, unwilted,
with silent shorelines,
                    until, prodded
by moonbeam, gaze, or gale,
                              it ruffles. After rising
from bark it follows
                    another leaf's fall,
breaks from its branch
the way in the sea's successions a wave
accumulates,
              rising from the chill fathoms,
until when laden it crouches
over itself,
              tumbling summit
to base, recto to verso, iris to eyelid,
flickering like some beacon,
                              isolate and imminent.
Like a hammock from which someone
has risen, it billows—
                    then rumbles to shore,
gilds the ground, where
it hunkers down and begins
                              that deeper descent,
folding at the margins,
                    foaming along the edges,

flecked with brown (the way the grass
was flecked by the leaf's shadow)

                              then conceding
a sheer surface, under which appear
bubbles and pebbles—

                    a sea spume, a damp detritus.
When I convey what is left,
it collapses in my hand,

                    and then my hand collapses.

Gravity

takes under its wing a horseshoe,
apple, the moon, bonds page
to table, head to
cushion, contriving a whirl-
pool, a spinning world,
so that in water a penitence,

in glass a mayhem, in pendulums
constancy. Our love
appoints its kingdom,
but gravity does not elect
or refrain; it effects
its spell over hammer and feather

alike, pebble and petal,
so each at the same rate
falls. And baptismal
it can carry straight away
lofting in a wave
an entire person, whispers and all

converted to a thud on the wet
bathroom floor. Tired after
work, too much weight
bearing down on one knee,
the entire body
carousels, a tilting and jilted mass,

fluttering as pinion as hum
as smoke rising from
                    a candelabrum.
        The arms, effervescent, flare
                    toward the sink, then the floor—
to break the fall with the body's own.

        To bend to one's will, we often
say, but what if
                    the will is already bent?
        As I walk out of Alesci's,
                    my bag of groceries
rips open. To hunch is to orbit,

        to bend shadowy over tiles—
skin, hair, and sleeves
                    bulbous as the tides.
        Even at my most poised,
                    I am superposed—
placed on the verge of entering

        or exceeding the earth,
revolving around an ever-
                    revolving orb, both
        of us circling one of the
                    many bright minutiae
in the universe, that dark effusion

        boundless but still to an extent
suggestive of embrace.
                    There are no fragments,
        only wrinkles. When I hit
                    the carpet,
do not walk over me. Please hear.

On a Line by Proust

Silent now, the yellow house with its host
of hiding places is gray. *The true paradises*
are the paradises that we have lost.

We threw the geese bread, stiff as toast,
crenellating the loaf; we watered the irises.
Those days are silent now. Without a host

the herb garden is overgrown. Like a ghost
mint lingers on the ground. Rosemary, basil, chives
were my paradises. I have lost

the rows that stretched, when as the tallest
I strode before the class—or toward the apse,
where into the silence the priest raised the host

above his head. And now like the Eucharist,
(like madeleine-laden tea) the taste of Orange Julius
contains the paradises we have lost.

Those who called at me call from bed, dear Proust,
or turn away to peck at sleep. Their memories
are silent now, and I, the only host
of the paradises we have lost.

Knot in the Wood

ingrown shadow   dark that won't dislodge

thud   in the amber   ringed planet

conundrum   cold lucifer   robed

in orbits   vinyl record   that seems

to spin   its music wafting   through the wood

a tide pool   amid shorelines   anemone in water

my once upon   that I wonder on   my plot

where I plowed   unfolded   leaving

a garnish   sliced lemon   ghostbranch

memorial   to dogged leaf   and sway

to the wind's cool   skirmishes

the grain ruffled   like a fleet of sails   look

one   has shipwrecked   the wood

is weakest   here   where it remembers

The Phone Call

The ringing woke me up.
It took awhile to realize
what was being said.

I started shivering. The room
couldn't be bothered—
not even the flinch of a curtain

by the open window.
I tried to scribble it down—
names of avenues, breeds of grass—

the dark ink chiseling away.
—Finally, I ran one fierce
line across the page.

It would be hours till daylight.
I was alone and had been living
that way for quite some time.

Perch

I'll stay here a bit longer, breathe deep
and let the gardenia
sketch my portrait
                with its fragrance.
The sunlight levels by early evening—
crowds gathering
                beneath marquees.
The goth kids entreat me with cups
of change, and neon reflects on
the wet street the way memory shimmers—
dim and bloated.
                I do not feel wronged,
only a lightness. Dusk
tosses its gravel
                straight through me.

                * * * * *

Where's the moonless white?
Where's the loss
                not pollinated by grief?
Leaves leak from
the dogwoods, and shadows ensnare
the side of a building
                like shoots of dark ivy.

                * * * * *

It would be nice to think, what if things
were different,

                  but the imagination
grows careless
and drafty when stretched

                          over broad expanses.
The robins fly, hasty,
moon-sharpened,

                    exhaled from the branches.
Only sometimes they perch
before us, uninhibited, their plumes trailing
farther than we thought

                      they could reach.

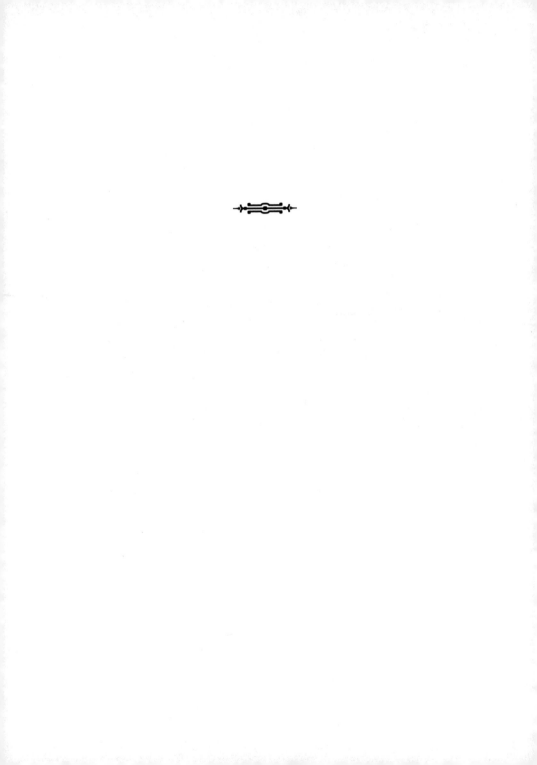

Incurable Cloud

Don't know why, but the dog is barking.
Rain pesters the roof,
faint but incessant, like shame.
In the dark I see the tall posts
but not the wire fence that separates
the vineyard from the road.
The eyes are not doors. They
are small containers.
They cannot hold the moon,
but they hold its flare.
They cannot hold the departed,
but they hold their names—
Dom, Julius, Caroline.
Under a balcony, where it is dry,
someone has dragged two chairs
and left them. Fallen
from the elms, leaves curl
into empty cups, pale basins.
I cannot love what doesn't
fret or crumble or grow cold.
I cannot bear to love what does.
Wind rummages through the screen.
Lying under a blanket, I close
one eye. The room closes the other.

Half the Leaves

Half the leaves press the grass
                        to keep the earth at bay.
Half the leaves are raised to halt the sky.

Paint peels from the pale column of the gazebo.
On the watermelon
               flies constellate.

We feed apples and carrots to the horses
over the fence. I pluck their hairs from the barbed wire.

A poised moth
               fans its wings like an oak
casting a shadow, enfolds them like an oak at noon.

These teeth that can only be white or whiter.
These bones
            that can only break or brace.

How the mouth makes a moon
               when we say *moon*.

What We Know

We live in a house on the edge
of the city. Dust coats
the floor and windows,
slumbers inside our clothes—
almost divine, the way
it gets into everything.
Our porch looks out
onto slow clouds and the halos
of sprinklers, shade pushed
to the corners of the lawns.
When it storms at night, lightning
disfigures the darkness.
We eat with spots on
the silverware. Feeling
the crevices with our tongues,
we lick the plates,
cold and chipped, clean.
We walk with our shirts unbuttoned—
the rooms without curtains.
Our lungs flutter furtively
whenever we pass an open window.
Our scars slowly sink back
beneath our skin—
little pursed lips holding their secrets.
Our tears, like our hair and nails,
have broken off from us
and stopped beating.

What we've learned of love
we keep in a narrow closet
beneath the stairs, wrapped
in tissue so it will not wrinkle.
What we've lost swims
under the surfaces of mirrors.
Sometimes we burn our stories
page by page in the oven.
Sometimes we leave them
by the curb at night
like an old armoire.
Sometimes we prop open
the front door, let the breeze reach
through the house, lie down
and tell them to each
other, over and over.
Touch me on the shoulder,
and it means *memory*;
touch me on the elbow,
and it means *come follow*—

A Thousand Small Nights

Each with its own moon, and its own darkness
brooding like an eyelid
above the pale crescent.
                         I brush the twigs
from the porch table
and watch the first stars
                               seize hold of the sky.
In the kitchen, you
scoop cantaloupe into cool orbs.
The body in love
                  is like a jar of fireflies—

salt, sequins,
                      a sudden fit of rain, a bottle
of peroxide
                  that still froths, the doorknob
that floats in the hall
                        like a stud earring—
what gifts there are arrive on occasion
and fit inside the hand.

Above the dark precipice of trees,
an airplane stencils its path
                          across the sky.
Like beads of an abacus,
                      headlights slide
over the ridge. Not the color of your eyes,
but when they close.

Light-Footed

The light has been walked over. It lies
in cinders where rain has gathered
                              inside tire tracks.
It cannot be put back.
Along the edge of the road, where the children
walk, skirting puddles,
grass presses
            to the ground, whispering.

The light isn't only lit. The light
waves, the light sits and weights, the light houses,
and the spot
            lights: a shady node, coffee
and crackers, granite
                    skirted with leaf.

Later in the kitchen I cook with the radio on—
garlic resonating from my hands.

The dog jumps up and puts his paws on the front
of my hips,
            and all three of us billow

together. As we sway, mud from the hike
to Millcreek
                uncakes from our feet
and under our weight disseminates, a pollen,
a few notes
                stomped from the staff,

                                a powder.

Call it *low tide*, call it *milky way*, call it
slow motion.
                What does it matter?
In the morning I'll rise early and sweep the room.

Reflections

iris by the side of the house inside of which I rest

＊＊＊＊＊

on a moonlit summer night under the sunlit moon

＊＊＊＊＊

feathers are in the air a feat of theirs

＊＊＊＊＊

parents in the train window winnowed to transparence

in a fog of forgetfulness they forget the fullness of fog

＊ ＊ ＊ ＊ ＊

the bouquet gives way wind torn wind borne away the gift of a bouquet

＊ ＊ ＊ ＊ ＊

once our memory of it darkens we'll no longer remember the dark

＊ ＊ ＊ ＊ ＊

I touch you not to spar but to spare your touch

to gather the pieces and piece them together

to turn to each other and hover between terms

and gently nest the shores of a shared emptiness

The Shards Still Trembling

As the parade goes by the park,
the woman next to me says
to her husband, *I just want to hear*

the bagpipes and then we can go.
You still appear to me in my sleep,
although it's never really you.

Pregnant and iridescent, you
watch television—the door
to your motel room cracked open.

Then you're the breath
on the other end of the telephone
saying, *I always knew—*

or the old man in the bodega
on the corner trying to strike
a deal for a rotting plum.

I walk with the crowd, past lucid curtains
and the passion of laundromats.
Alone so long, I am everyone.

When I lived by the casino,
we'd walk down the crumbling steps
to the beach at night and listen

to the ocean tearing blue page after
blue page from its journal.
Fishermen drank and listened

to a mandolin strumming—their lines
fidgeting in the water.
Fish quivered in buckets of ice.

I was not born in that country.
We sat on a bench, intertwined—
the flushed sky slowly abating.

I said in my native tongue, *ring,*
thumb—and touched your
knuckle, your nail. *Temple.*

I could make you shudder
with the simplest words.

Hush

It is the quiet that comes
after, a ladle of chill. Silence,

from shore to sheer shore, spans,
but hush lodges,

inland. Hush, like a locket,
encloses, and lets no sentiment spill.

Without hush, there'd be no shrapnel
in belltoll or wingbeat—

and without the summons
of a trill, there would be no hush.

The calm after a quake
is no calmer. Covering up

quickly, it resonates and wounds.
A silence has nothing to hide, but hush

approaches and says, *now don't cry.*
In the beginning there was *us*—

then up spumed two lassitudes,
gust-filled gulfs, one on each

side, thin hollows, where air
flocks only to flatten. *Hush.*

You sighed first. I followed.

Like the Touch of Bent Grass

The slightest regret smells
of folded gloves or unpoured water—

the slightest love lingers on
like a mirror
                    flashed into a mirror.

At night sheets tangle on the beds
around bodies or guitars.

We live not with what never happened
but with what came close

to happening.
                    The way the blade
of a sundial casts a revolving shadow,

like a sail that as the wind dwindles
drapes to nothingness, then

as the wind blows
                    slowly blooms,
unveiling an apex—

each event in this quiet
crumble is gilded
                    by satellites.

Clearing, Clear

                         —not the field so much as the deer
sensing a presence and crossing, not crossing so much
as turning and setting their tails in motion,
flickering behind them, not the tip
of the flame so much as the width, the way it bulges
like a vase or a pair of hips
and tapers, as if it might be called upon to give
birth, the way the cottonwood, heavy,
lowers its branches and then raises them
after the blossoms fall, not the field so much as the cottonwood,
leafless, in the middle of the pasture, not divested
of leaf so much as divulging its branches to the white sky,
knotted like a fingerprint
on a mirror or a wine glass raised at someone's confirmation,
which, though not comprehended, the finger
presses and marks, piping its fitful
lines onto the surface, a meringue shell, a single
memory, a little gastropod in clear water,
                                                but not
the cottonwood so much as the sky
behind it, the clouds, thin and shrill, that portend
slowly, as if snagged but wafting in the blue
skybrook, then tarry, listless
as the cattle that graze beneath them and huddle in the ribbons
of shade beneath a single tree, not listless so much
as resolved, in complaint against the wind that
chills their nostrils and ruffles

the dry grass, unbuffeted, at the edge of the field, or rather
not the edge of the field but the beginning, the way the shore
is not only the edge of a lake but its
brim, the force against which the lake coheres, clearing,
clear, so that the bathers will come, place their
keys and glasses inside their shoes,
their shoes on the dock, and plunge into the murky
water, flourishing their arms as if carving out
angels in a constant cascade
of snow, moving but never overcoming the water's
one ambition to fall
into the spaces they leave behind them,
                                        no, not the edge
of the lake so much as the brim, the water
repelled by the shore, the way a shadow is cast by the figure,
upright, that shuns it, not so much shuns
as interposes, the way the storm clouds interpose between sun
and pasture, and, even though the clouds
whiten like hesitations, their shadows on the grass
deepen the emerald, while on box elders unfurl
buds that within a month suspend the rain in their leafy
folds, so that when wafted
in the wind, the trees, as if they were clouds, sputter,
releasing droplets of water, and thunder, cavernous,
echoes, and the deer scatter
across the field, but not crossing
so much as turning and setting their tails in motion—

Plea for Interlude

I only ask that there are moments when the sponge,
desiccate, rests on the counter like an empty pedestal,

when the floors are swept bare, and rain is held
in the leaves like a letter written but never sent,

—furrows of grace—when the knife sits by the bread,
the pink salmon is consumed by white paper, and

the ring shimmers beside the sink, forced from
its finger—the hovering hour—when the last sheet,

so vast it takes more than one to fold, lies flat
in the cupboard, so that only a spider on the sill

insists, and, while the windows turn so dark they
become doors, my breath erupts into my breaths.

Rain

Along the road, palm fronds paddle in the violent rain.
Then they rest, pendulous, in a faint rain.

Between the hills alights an iridescent arc.
We stop washing mangos and point at the lucent rain.

An umbrella screens a man's shirt, but his pants
darken as he walks. Why do you tell it slant, rain?

I can't sleep. The dog warbles—the moon strays.
I want to lie under shadows and a resonant rain.

Like bread and fish, a single drop proliferates.
You need one more miracle to be a saint, rain.

I wear the same orange shirt to work each and every day.
It hangs on the line, and I hope it won't rain.

Some clouds are locomotive; others lie like tracks—
thin rails that shine and sprinkle a scant rain.

They are all at the other house when the thunder strikes.
I microwave some rice and listen to you chant, rain.

The cows find refuge under a tree, except for one,
who continues to graze. You have a new tenant, rain.

The ferns turn to claws, and the dirt road clenches
chunks of granite. The farmers await the truant rain.

God said to Adam: *Now your rib is carrion.*
Go to the fields and bend in the intermittent rain.

For Nashaly

Already a cough roosts in your chest—
already shadows partition
the room and the voice that sings to you
forgets the words and hums.

Fourteen months since
your birth, and as you lie on the sofa only your eyes
gesticulate. Already hibiscus

stoops by the roadside, dust-dangled.
The fields resound with stridulations of crickets—
the hills torched with mist.

Although you're not my daughter,
your cough still chides.
I'd cut the dampness right out of this blanket,
but then it wouldn't hold you.

Beside the house you've wandered among Coke bottles,
scuttling chickens, and clotheslines
dappled with socks
and sweaters, between red earth and hatching rain.

There's no beginning or end to any of this,
only a paleness where
sleep is quenched—or hair is parted.

The shirts, drying, rise in the wind.
A white moth flutters through the yard—
a tremulous hinge.

The Opposite of Sugar

the opposite of sugar isn't salt

       a pinch of salt and the green mango

the opposite of the hand isn't the foot

       a hand to cover the groin

the opposite of heavy isn't light

       pink evening light through the screen

the opposite of right isn't left

       pecking at what's left

the opposite of grant isn't refuse

       Styrofoam refuse

the opposite of the sun isn't the moon

       quarter moon like a white hare

the opposite of here isn't there

       there there, child, there there

NOTES

"Hydrangea" is informed by Toni Lawson-Hall and Brian Rothera's *Hydrangeas: A Gardener's Guide* (Portland: Timber Press, 2005).

"Porcupine" is informed by Uldis Roze's *The North American Porcupine* (Ithaca: Cornell UP, 2009).

"Garland" is after C. D. Wright's "Lake Echo, Dear."

"Orchids, Avenues" is after Philip Larkin's "Places, Loved Ones."

"On a Line by Proust" is after Eleanor Stanford's "On a Line by Petrarch."

"Reflections" is partially inspired by Unica Zürn's anagram poems.

1987   Elton Glaser, *Tropical Depressions*
       Michael Pettit, *Cardinal Points*

1988   Bill Knott, *Outremer*
       Mary Ruefle, *The Adamant*

1989   Conrad Hilberry, *Sorting the Smoke*
       Terese Svoboda, *Laughing Africa*

1990   Philip Dacey, *Night Shift at the Crucifix Factory*
       Lynda Hull, *Star Ledger*

1991   Greg Pape, *Sunflower Facing the Sun*
       Walter Pavlich, *Running near the End of the World*

1992   Lola Haskins, *Hunger*
       Katherine Soniat, *A Shared Life*

1993   Tom Andrews, *The Hemophiliac's Motorcycle*
       Michael Heffernan, *Love's Answer*
       John Wood, *In Primary Light*

1994   James McKean, *Tree of Heaven*
       Bin Ramke, *Massacre of the Innocents*
       Ed Roberson, *Voices Cast Out to Talk Us In*

1995   Ralph Burns, *Swamp Candles*
       Maureen Seaton, *Furious Cooking*

1996   Pamela Alexander, *Inland*
       Gary Gildner, *The Bunker in the Parsley Fields*
       John Wood, *The Gates of the Elect Kingdom*